Helen Keller
A Determined Life

written by Elizabeth MacLeod

Kids Can Press

In memory of my daughter, Barbara, whose love for others made a difference. I miss her. — Pamela Shellington

Consultant: Jan Seymour-Ford

Acknowledgments

Very special thanks to Jan Seymour-Ford, Research Librarian, Perkins School for the Blind, for reviewing the manuscript so carefully and for being extremely helpful in so many ways.

I really appreciate the team that has worked so hard to create this book. It is a real pleasure to work with two such terrific editors, Chris McClymont and Val Wyatt — many, many thanks to you both. I am also very grateful for all the creativity, effort and time Karen Powers has put into the design of this book. Patricia Buckley is an extremely persistent and skilled photo researcher and has worked so hard to gather the book's images. Thanks also to Barbara Spurll for creating such wonderful illustrations of Helen.

Thanks always to Dad, John and Douglas. And special thanks to Paul for opening my eyes and ears to so many wonderful things.

Kids Can Press acknowledges the financial support of the Government of Ontario, through the Ontario Media Development Corporation's Ontario Book Initiative; the Ontario Arts Council; the Canada Council for the Arts; and the Government of Canada, through the BPIDP, for our publishing activity.

Published in Canada by
Kids Can Press Ltd.
29 Birch Avenue
Toronto, ON M4V 1E2

Published in the U.S. by
Kids Can Press Ltd.
2250 Military Road
Tonawanda, NY 14150

www.kidscanpress.com

Series editor: Valerie Wyatt
Edited by Christine McClymont
Designed by Karen Powers
Printed in Hong Kong, China, by Wing King Tong

The hardcover edition of this book is smyth sewn casebound.
The paperback edition of this book is limp sewn with a drawn-on cover.

CM 04 0 9 8 7 6 5 4 3 2 1
CM PA 04 0 9 8 7 6 5 4 3 2 1

National Library of Canada Cataloguing in Publication Data

MacLeod, Elizabeth
    Helen Keller : a determined life / written by Elizabeth MacLeod.

Includes index.

ISBN 1-55337-508-4 (bound).   ISBN 1-55337-509-2 (pbk.)

1. Keller, Helen, 1880–1968 — Juvenile literature. 2. Sullivan, Annie, 1866–1936 — Juvenile literature. 3. Blind-deaf women — United States — Biography — Juvenile literature. I. Title.

HV1624.K4M33 2004   j362.4'1'092   C2003-903497-6

Photo credits

Every reasonable effort has been made to trace ownership of and give accurate credit to copyrighted material. Information that would enable the publisher to correct any discrepancies in future editions would be appreciated.

Abbreviations
t = top; b = bottom; c = center; l = left; r = right

Alexander Graham Bell Association for the Deaf and Hard of Hearing: back cover (trc), 17 (b). **Photos courtesy of the American Foundation for the Blind. Used with permission of the American Foundation for the Blind, Helen Keller Archives:** back cover (cr), 1, 3 (bl, ct, cb), 4, 6, 7 (br), 9 (tr), 13 (ct), 15 (tr), 17 (l, t), 18, 19 (l, t, c), 21 (tl, bl), 22 (t), 23 (bl), 25, 26, 27 (t, c), 28, 29 (tr, cr). **Frank Baldaserra:** 7 (bl), 9 (br), 22 (b). **Chicago Historical Society:** 15 (tl). **Circus World Museum, Baraboo, Wisconsin/B&B NL38093-IF-7:** 12. **Alison Wright/Magma/Corbis:** 29 (cl). **Creatas:** 13 (t). **Franklin D. Roosevelt Library:** 24. **Getty Images:** 29(tl). **Larry Gillentine:** 7(t). **The Hadley School for the Blind:** front cover (b), 15 (br). **Library of Congress:** front cover (c), back cover (cl), 5 (b), 9 (bl), 14, 16, 20. **Photos courtesy of Perkins School for the Blind:** front cover (t), back cover (tl, tc, tr), 3 (t, br), 5 (t), 8, 10, 11 (r,b), 13 (cb, b), 15 (bl), 17 (c), 21 (tr, br), 23 (tr), 27 (b). **Smithsonian Institute, National Numismatic Collection:** 23(br). **Society for the Preservation of New England Antiquities (negative #50795-A):** 11(t). **Tewksbury Historical Society, photo by David Marcus:** 11(l). **Toronto Reference Library:** 23(tl).

Kids Can Press is a *Corus*™ Entertainment company

Contents

Meet Helen Keller

Helen traveled the world, making people more aware of vision loss and raising money to help blind and deaf people. Wherever she toured, such as Australia in 1948, crowds flocked to see her.

When Helen was seven, she learned to write. The writing was called "square-hand script" because of the shape of the letters.

Imagine not being able to communicate with anyone. You couldn't say how you were feeling or what you wanted. How incredibly frustrating! Helen Keller knew that frustration. Before she was two years old, a terrible illness left her deaf and blind. But thanks to her courage and determination, Helen learned to communicate. Her struggles and triumphs still inspire people around the world.

Called America's First Lady of Courage, a national treasure and one of the most important people of the 20th century, Helen became the first deaf-blind person ever to graduate from college. She also traveled to many countries as an author, lecturer and fundraiser.

Helen fought for the rights of women and minorities and encouraged people with disabilities everywhere. Along the way, she met many famous people and a lot of them became her good friends. They were drawn to Helen's sense of humor and bright smile.

Helen's story is also the story of Annie Sullivan, the wonderful teacher who unlocked the door of communication for Helen and brought her out of her silent darkness. Annie became known as "The Miracle Worker" because she broke through to Helen's mind and taught her the magic of language. Annie spent almost her whole life at Helen's side, helping Helen experience the world around her.

How was Helen able to communicate with people? What made her so determined? How did she become one of the world's most important champions of people with disabilities?

"The world is moved along not by the mighty shoves of a few, but the tiny pushes of each individual."
— Helen

Helen Keller

Many deaf people use American Sign Language (ASL) to communicate, but Helen used a one-hand manual alphabet. She formed words with one hand and used the other hand to feel what the other person was signing.

A B C D E F G H I J K L M N O P Q R S T U V W X Y Z

The First Appearance on the Lecture Platform of

HELEN KELLER

And her Teacher Mrs. Macy (Anne M. Sullivan)

"The Heart and the Ha

TREMONT
ONE NI
MONDAY EVENING,
SEATS. 25c. to

Making money was a constant struggle for Helen — in the early 1900s governments and organizations didn't help people with disabilities as much as they do now. With Annie's help, Helen earned money telling audiences about her life.

Although Helen couldn't see or hear, she could feel vibrations — from the "round thump," as she called it, of a pencil rolling on the floor to the crash of a falling tree.

I had strong senses of smell and taste and lived in a world rich in sensations.

Young Helen

Arthur Henley Keller had been a captain in the army for the southern states during the American Civil War (1861–1865). By the time Helen was born, he was a newspaper editor. His two sons from an earlier marriage, James and Simpson, were much older than their half sister Helen.

Helen's mother, Kate Adams Keller, was almost 20 years younger than her husband. She was smart and hardworking and, like Helen, very determined.

Captain Arthur Keller and his wife, Kate, were delighted with their smart, beautiful daughter, born in 1880. By the time Helen was just six months old, she was already saying, "How do you do?" — or so her father proudly claimed. Not only was she walking when she was one, she was almost running, declared her mother.

But tragedy struck when Helen became deathly ill at the age of 19 months. For days, she lay sick and sweating while her frantic parents struggled to keep her alive. The doctor said she had "acute congestion of the stomach and brain" and he expected her to die. Today, experts think Helen may have suffered from encephalitis, a disease that causes high fevers and swelling in the brain. Or she may have had scarlet fever or meningitis, two other illnesses that cause high fevers.

Helen's parents were overjoyed when Helen's temperature suddenly dropped and she began to recover. But they soon discovered that the illness had made their daughter completely deaf. Since Helen couldn't hear people talking, she soon wasn't able to speak, either.

Her parents also noticed that Helen found any light too bright, and that her left eye had swelled and become deformed. Gradually, Helen lost her sight and became blind. Much later, she said that she felt like a ghost or a prisoner. "I cannot remember how I felt when the light went out of my eyes," said Helen. "I suppose I thought it was always night and perhaps I wondered why day did not come."

Helen's parents were devastated. At that time, blindness still terrified people, and those who couldn't hear were treated as if they were stupid. What kind of life could possibly lie ahead for their beloved daughter, who was suddenly both deaf and blind?

"Then came the illness which closed my eyes and ears and plunged me into the unconsciousness of a newborn baby." — Helen

TENNESSEE

● Tuscumbia

ALABAMA

GEORGIA

FLORIDA

Ivy Green, the Keller plantation, got its name from the ivy that covered many of the buildings. Helen was born in this little cottage close to the main house.

When I was born on June 27, 1880, in Tuscumbia, Alabama, fewer than 2000 people lived there and almost everyone knew my family.

After her terrible illness, Helen lived in a silent, dark world. She couldn't understand what had happened to the sounds and colors she loved, but she got some comfort from patting her furry little dog.

One summer day, Helen and a friend sat cutting paper dolls. When they got bored with that, they began chopping up their shoelaces, then their hair. Mrs. Keller showed up just before Helen lost her curls!

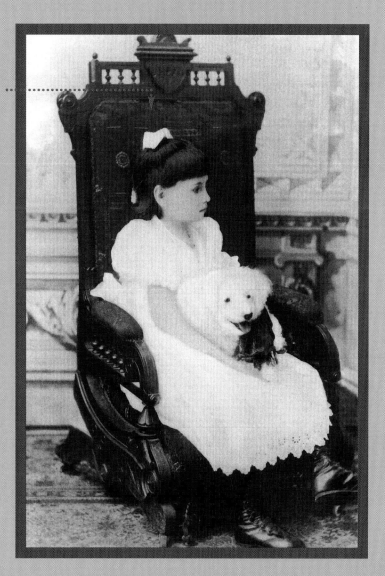

Darkness

Helen was five when her sister, Mildred (below), was born. One day, Helen found her baby sister in Helen's doll cradle. She was so angry that she overturned the cradle. Luckily, Mrs. Keller was close enough to catch Mildred as she fell.

"I stood between two persons who were conversing and touched their lips …
I moved my lips and gesticulated frantically without result. This made me so angry at times that I kicked and screamed until I was exhausted."
— Helen

Helen laughed as she leaned against the pantry door. She couldn't hear her mother yelling for her to unlock it, but she could feel the vibrations from her pounding. It took three hours before Mrs. Keller was released.

No wonder most of the Kellers' servants and visitors felt Helen was unmanageable. She broke lamps and dishes and threw terrible temper tantrums. Helen screamed and kicked like a wild pony when she couldn't communicate — that earned her the nickname "Little Bronco."

But Helen's parents knew she was smart. She made up about 60 signs to represent her family and her favorite foods. For instance, she pretended to put on glasses as a sign to mean her father, and she shivered when she wanted ice cream. When she was five, she could fold and put away laundry and always knew which clothes were hers.

Doctor after doctor said that nothing could be done to help Helen. Some suggested she go to an institution for children with physical disabilities. However, Helen's parents knew that she'd receive almost no education there. They still dreamed of something better for their daughter.

When Helen was six, Mrs. Keller found an interesting book by Charles Dickens, author of *A Christmas Carol.* In it Dickens described his meeting with Laura Bridgman, a young girl who was deaf-blind and had learned to communicate. The story filled Mrs. Keller with hope — couldn't Helen learn, too?

Captain Keller was doubtful. After all, the book was more than 40 years old and Laura's school, the Perkins Institution for the Blind, was in faraway Boston. But Mrs. Keller wouldn't give up. Eventually the Captain compromised: he would take Helen to one more eye doctor.

But the doctor in Baltimore couldn't offer a cure for Helen's blindness. Instead, he suggested that they visit Alexander Graham Bell, who lived in nearby Washington, D.C. You may know Dr. Bell as the inventor of the telephone, but he was also famous as a teacher of deaf people. If Helen couldn't be cured, perhaps she could be taught.

Dr. Bell found Helen's face "chillingly empty," but he was impressed with how clever she was. He told the Kellers to ask Michael Anagnos, head of the Perkins Institution, to help find a teacher for Helen. Mr. Anagnos instantly thought of a young woman with as much fighting spirit as Helen. Her name was Annie Sullivan.

Helen touched and smelled everything, including leaves and flowers.

When Helen met Alexander Graham Bell, he took her on his knee and made his watch chime for her. She was delighted because she could feel the vibrations.

Even as a little girl, I could recognize people by feeling their faces and clothes.

Alexander Graham Bell and Helen would be friends all their lives. He quickly recognized how bright she was, and she felt how much he loved her.

If Helen wanted a piece of bread, she imitated cutting a slice and spreading butter on it.

"Miss Spitfire" Sullivan

"The most important day I remember in all my life is the one on which my teacher came to me." — Helen

Annie's childhood was so miserable that it would be almost 50 years before she could talk about it. Here she is at age 15, about a year after she began studying at the Perkins Institution for the Blind and six years before she met Helen.

It's hard to imagine a worse childhood than Annie Sullivan's. She was born in 1866 to a very poor family in Feeding Hills (part of Agawam), Massachusetts. When she was five, she got trachoma, a disease that caused hard lumps inside her eyelids. These lumps nearly destroyed her vision.

Annie threw fierce temper tantrums, and her father beat her to control her. Her mother tried to protect her, but she died when Annie was about eight. In 1876, Annie and her brother, Jimmie, were sent to the poorhouse in Tewksbury, Massachusetts.

There, the pair lived in filth among poor, sick or mentally ill people. Despite the rats and cockroaches, Annie wasn't unhappy. She could play with Jimmie — even though their playroom was the "dead house" where corpses were readied for burial. But Jimmie soon died and Annie was alone.

One day, a government group came to inspect the poorhouse. Annie followed the men, trying to find the courage to speak to them. As they were about to leave, she finally yelled to them, "I want to go to school!" Her desperation touched the committee, and so the men arranged for her to attend the Perkins Institution for the Blind in Boston.

Annie was almost 14 when she arrived at Perkins, but she couldn't read or write. At first the other pupils, as well as some teachers, made fun of her. She reacted by talking back rudely and earned the nickname "Miss Spitfire." But slowly, she began to make friends, including Laura Bridgman (page 8). Most importantly, Annie learned the one-hand manual alphabet (page 5) so that she could "talk" with deaf-blind Laura.

While Annie was at Perkins, her eyes were operated on a number of times. Her vision improved, although her eyes would always be weak and sore. When she graduated in 1886, she was head of her class. But, she wondered, what would she do now?

A few months later, Mr. Anagnos, the head of Perkins, received Captain Keller's request for a teacher for Helen. He thought Annie would be perfect. Annie was pleased, but wasn't sure she could do it. So she spent six months preparing and learning about her friend Laura's education.

After a two-day train ride, with eyes sore from another operation, Annie arrived at the Kellers' home on March 3, 1887. Helen rushed at her and almost knocked her over. What an introduction to the girl whose life Annie would change completely!

Tewksbury ●

MASSACHUSETTS

● Agawam
(Feeding Hills)

CONNECTICUT

● Boston

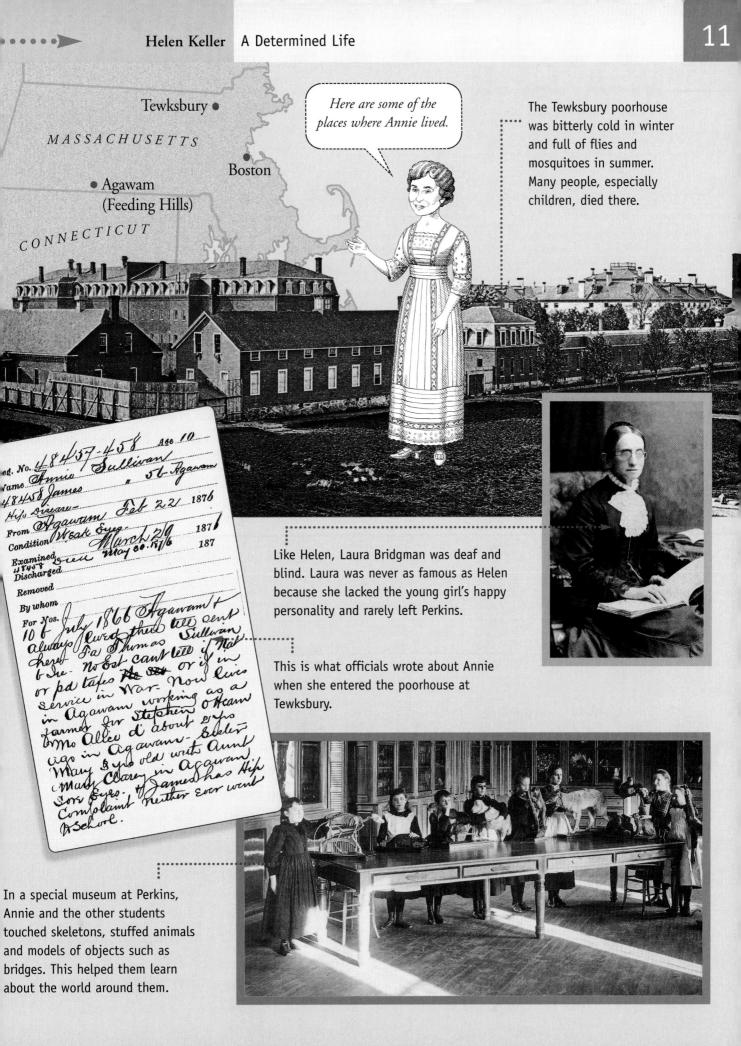

Here are some of the places where Annie lived.

The Tewksbury poorhouse was bitterly cold in winter and full of flies and mosquitoes in summer. Many people, especially children, died there.

Like Helen, Laura Bridgman was deaf and blind. Laura was never as famous as Helen because she lacked the young girl's happy personality and rarely left Perkins.

This is what officials wrote about Annie when she entered the poorhouse at Tewksbury.

In a special museum at Perkins, Annie and the other students touched skeletons, stuffed animals and models of objects such as bridges. This helped them learn about the world around them.

W-A-T-E-R

"I left the well house eager to learn. Everything had a name, and each name gave birth to a new thought. As we returned to the house, every object I touched seemed to quiver with life."
— Helen

About eight months after Annie arrived in Tuscumbia, she took Helen to the circus. The little girl was delighted to feed the elephants, pat the leopard and laugh at the monkeys who tried to steal the flowers from her hat.

Almost as soon as Annie met Helen, she began spelling words into the little girl's hands using the one-hand manual alphabet. Helen copied the shapes back to Annie, but they meant nothing to her. Still, Helen's ability to repeat the letters so easily showed how smart she was.

Annie quickly realized she must also teach Helen discipline. For one thing, during one of her tantrums, Helen knocked out two of Annie's teeth. For another, when the family ate its meals, Helen walked around picking food off people's plates. One morning, Annie made everyone leave the dining room while she taught Helen some manners. Helen kicked and screamed but Annie persevered, and Helen finally learned to sit still and eat with a spoon.

Annie saw how Helen's family spoiled her. She thought she could make a lot more progress with Helen if she got her away from them. So teacher and pupil moved into a small cottage on the farm for a few weeks. Annie gained more control over Helen, and the little girl quickly learned obedience and patience.

Despite Helen's progress, Annie was discouraged. Nothing Annie tried helped her pupil understand the idea of names and language. One morning in early April, Helen was having trouble understanding the difference between "mug" and "water." Annie kept spelling the letters into Helen's hand, but still the little girl was confused. Annie wracked her brain trying to think of another way to break through to Helen.

Then Annie had an idea — the water pump. They ran outside, and Helen held her mug under the spout while Annie pumped. As the water gushed out, Annie spelled "W-A-T-E-R" into Helen's hand. Helen suddenly dropped her mug and, as Annie said, "A new light came into her face." Helen had finally connected the finger movements with names. By the end of the day, she had learned 30 new words. Her parents were so grateful to Annie. What a change in Helen in only one month!

To teach Helen more words, Annie "talked" to Helen all the time, just as parents do with young children. Soon Helen was finger-spelling sentences. In May, Annie began teaching her to read. At first Helen's books had large letters that were raised enough that she could feel them. A little later, she learned braille, a system of writing that uses raised dots for letters and numbers (it's named for its inventor, Louis Braille). Now that she could communicate, Helen was fired with a desire to learn.

Annie had spelled W-A-T-E-R into Helen's hands many times but on April 5, 1887, Helen said, "I stood still, my whole attention fixed upon the motions of her fingers. Suddenly I felt a misty consciousness as of something forgotten … and somehow the mystery of language was revealed to me."

As the water flowed over my hands, I finally connected the cool liquid with the letters Annie was spelling.

W A T E R

At first Helen didn't understand what finger-spelling meant, but that didn't stop her from trying to teach one of the family's dogs how to make letters. She even finger-spelled in her sleep!

When Helen asked Annie for her name, she spelled "Teacher" into Helen's hand. Helen called Annie "Teacher" for the rest of her life.

Away to school

Mark Twain, author of *Tom Sawyer,* thought it was ridiculous that Helen was accused of plagiarism (pretending to have written something that someone else wrote). He called her judges "a collection of decayed turnips." Twain nicknamed Annie "The Miracle Worker," and later arranged for Helen's college expenses to be paid.

"We can do anything we want to do if we stick to it long enough." — Helen

During the next year, Annie began telling her pupil about the students at the Perkins Institution in Boston. Helen longed to meet other children who were blind. When Helen wrote to the school's head, Mr. Anagnos, to ask if she and Annie could visit, he quickly said yes — stories about Helen's amazing success were already in newspapers around the world.

Soon after they arrived at Perkins, Annie and Helen visited Annie's deaf-blind friend, Laura Bridgman, whose story had inspired Helen's mother. Laura immediately recognized Annie's touch. But she and Helen didn't get along — the older woman found eight-year-old Helen too rough.

With Annie's help, Helen stayed at Perkins for four years and studied French, math, poetry, science and other subjects. She was eager to talk as well, so in 1890 she began speech lessons at the nearby Horace Mann School for the Deaf.

When Helen was 11, she wrote a story called "The Frost King" and sent it to Mr. Anagnos. He was so impressed that he had it published. But soon he heard that Helen's story was very similar to one written years before. Helen quickly admitted her tale was similar, but said she hadn't meant to copy and couldn't remember reading the original story.

Mr. Anagnos was furious. He set up a panel of judges, who questioned Helen about the story for two hours. In the end, the judges found the frightened girl innocent of copying. But Helen never wrote more stories, and she eventually left Perkins.

In 1894, Helen went to the Wright-Humason School for the Deaf in New York. There her speech improved, although she never spoke clearly. She did learn to lip-read better. Many deaf people lip-read by watching a person's lips move. Helen couldn't do that. But by putting her fingers on a speaker's throat and lips, she could feel how they were moving.

Helen's father died when Helen was only 16. She found comfort in Swedenborgianism, a religion that followed the teachings of Emanuel Swedenborg, a Swedish scientist from the 1700s. It emphasized spirituality, and Helen said it made her feel the same as people who see and hear.

Now Helen had a new goal. She was determined to attend Radcliffe College, a top American university in Boston. It took three tough years of studying, but Helen finally took her Radcliffe College entrance exams in 1899. Nervously, she awaited the results.

> *At the fair, I touched a huge diamond and valuable statues so that I could "see" them. I was also invited to feel the Egyptian mummies — but I refused.*

Studying didn't occupy all of Helen's time. She loved to hike, especially through sweet-smelling flowers — lilies of the valley were her favorite. She also biked, rode horses, rowed, swam and played checkers.

In 1893, Alexander Graham Bell took Helen and Annie to the World's Fair in Chicago. Crowds stared as the famous little girl and the inventor strolled through the exhibits.

Helen was happy to meet other kids with visual impairments at Perkins and "talk" with them — she could finger-spell about 80 words per minute. This picture is unusual because you can see Helen's bulging left eye.

To write a note or story, Helen placed a piece of paper over a board that looked like a checkerboard, with the edges of the squares cut into it like grooves. Her right hand guided her left — she was left-handed — across the page as she wrote each letter inside a square.

College girl

"It was my right as well as my duty to complete my college career so as to demonstrate how doubly handicapped children could be developed."
— Helen

Helen's classmates at Radcliffe gave her this Boston terrier, which she named Phiz — phiz is short for physiognomy, another word for face, and Helen thought he had a very funny, homely one.

Helen was so exhausted when she finished Radcliffe College's entrance exams that she was sure she'd failed. She was delighted to find out that she'd passed and to receive her certificate of admission in July 1899.

But Radcliffe wanted her to attend special classes. Helen had her heart set on regular courses there — despite scholarship offers from other colleges. Later Helen explained, "… they didn't want me at Radcliffe and, being stubborn, I chose to override their objections." After a year of struggle, she became the first deaf-blind person to attend Radcliffe.

During classes, Annie sat at Helen's side, spelling lectures to her. Helen's hands were busy "listening" so she couldn't take notes — instead, she rushed home after class to jot down what she remembered. Luckily, Helen had an amazing memory. As she studied, she finger-spelled facts to herself that she wanted to recall.

Helen didn't make a lot of friends at Radcliffe. Most of the young women had never met a person who was deaf-blind and didn't know how to communicate with her. They were also a little in awe of her. Besides, she and Annie had to work late into the night trying to keep up with all her courses — English, philosophy, history, languages, economics and others.

In 1901, when Helen was in her second year, *Ladies' Home Journal* magazine asked her to write some articles about her life. It was hard for Helen to fit in this extra work, but she needed the money. Helen's schooling had been paid for by rich friends, but for the past ten years, she'd been very short of funds.

Writing was much harder than Helen expected. But a friend introduced her to editor John Macy, and with his help, Helen finished the articles. Later, she gathered them into a book, *The Story of My Life*, which she dedicated to Alexander Graham Bell. It's still in bookstores more than 100 years later. With the money Helen made, she and Annie bought a home in Wrentham, near Boston. John strung a wire around the yard that Helen could hold onto and go walking on her own.

Helen was delighted to graduate with honors from Radcliffe College. She was the first college graduate who was deaf-blind in the United States — and it would be 50 years before the next. But now she faced the important questions of what to do with her life and how to earn a living.

At age 24, Helen graduated from Radcliffe. She'd enjoyed learning about so many new subjects and felt that her writing had improved a lot.

Annie liked to find new places for Helen to study, even trees. Annie had to "read" many of Helen's books to her, which made Annie's eyes ache. So when Annie asked Helen if she'd like anything repeated, Helen usually said no, even if she really did.

A braille writer looks like a typewriter but has just six keys and a space bar. It marks a page with raised dots that blind people can feel and read.

I wrote my college essays on a braille writer, then typed them using a regular typewriter.

RADCLIFFE COLLEGE.

CERTIFICATE OF ADMISSION.

CAMBRIDGE, _July 4_ 1899.

Helen Adams Keller

...tted to the FRESHMAN CLASS in Radcliffe College.

Agnes Irwin
Dean of Radcliffe College.

...s Keller passed with credit in Advanced Latin

When Helen went to college, many people still felt that too much education wasn't good for women — some people even thought it might drive them insane!

New life and love

The future may have seemed uncertain to Helen, but her fame was definitely growing. When she, Annie and John Macy attended a special Helen Keller Day in St. Louis, Missouri, in October 1904, the crowds were uncontrollable. People snatched roses Helen was carrying and someone grabbed her hat for a souvenir.

But Helen wanted to be more than famous. She decided to devote her life to helping people who are blind and to writing about vision loss. People loved to read her words, even though her style was quite stiff. No wonder — Helen couldn't hear everyday conversation, and Annie often shortened what she spelled for speed. Still, Helen was able to earn a living with her writing.

John continued to help Helen edit her writing. Soon he and Annie fell in love, and married in 1905. The couple lived with Helen, as John knew that she couldn't be separated from her teacher. He even gave them almost the same nickname — "Bill" for Annie and "Billy" for Helen.

If you look at photos of Helen up to this point, you'll see that almost all of them show only her right side. That's because her left eye was so deformed. In 1910, Helen had both eyes replaced with glass ones. She looked even more beautiful and now her full face could be photographed.

Three years later, Annie's marriage began to fall apart — partly because John was spending Helen's money. To earn the income they desperately needed, Helen decided to go on a lecture tour. She would talk about happiness and the importance of all five senses. She'd also tackle topics such as votes for women and better conditions for people with disabilities. Annie would repeat Helen's words so the audience understood.

In 1913, Helen nervously began her first lecture. When her performance was over, she was sure she had failed. Then she felt the floor vibrating and realized the audience was applauding wildly. Her next appearances were all successful, but one night Annie collapsed, leaving Helen helpless. After that, they decided to hire Polly Thomson as an assistant.

In 1916, the three women hired journalist Peter Fagan to help them, and Peter and Helen fell in love. But Helen's mother felt that people who were disabled should never marry. She rushed Helen home to Tuscumbia. When the couple tried to elope, Helen's family stopped them. The last time they were to meet, Peter was scared off. Helen waited all night before sadly accepting she'd never see him again.

Polly Thomson was a great help to Helen and Annie. She looked after their money, scheduled their lecture tours — and taught Helen how to dance! Helen could feel the music's rhythm through her feet.

At first, Annie, John and I lived happily together in my house at Wrentham.

Helen tried to help with the housework around the Wrentham home by washing dishes and tidying the rooms. But she was kept too busy with requests to write more articles or to fundraise for charities that helped people who were deaf or blind.

Here are Helen, John Macy and Annie in 1914. John was amazed to discover that Helen "talked" to herself. "When she is walking up and down the hall or along the veranda," he said, "her hands go flying along beside her like a confusion of bird's wings."

"The brief love will remain in my life, a little island of joy surrounded by dark waters. I am glad that I have had the experience of being loved and desired." — Helen

A Token of Love

When I call you, Dear, to my mind,
Food for true Love I always find.

THE WORLD I LIVE IN

HELEN KELLER

Helen once said, "I can't imagine a man wanting to marry me. I should think it would seem like marrying a statue." She was surprised and very happy when Peter Fagan proposed to her.

In 1908 Helen published *The World I Live In* to help readers learn about her life and see the importance to her of smell, taste and touch.

Stage star!

Helen's lecture tour ended when people no longer wanted to hear what she had to say. She had been speaking out against war, but with World War I (1914–1918) raging in Europe, and America about to join the fight, some people thought she was unpatriotic.

Since Helen had no lecture fees coming in, she had to sell the farm at Wrentham. She, Annie and Polly moved to a smaller home in Forest Hills, near New York City. When Helen was asked to appear in a movie about her life, she jumped at the chance to draw attention to the needs of people with visual impairments — and to make some money.

Filming of the movie, called *Deliverance*, began in 1918. Helen found acting to be hard work. What did it mean, she wondered, when the director told her to "act natural"? As well, she found the thick movie makeup and bright film lighting hot and tiring.

Movie reviewers loved the film when it opened in 1919, but it was a flop with the public. The war had just ended and people wanted funny movies. After months of work, Helen earned very little money — she had to borrow enough to get home to Forest Hills.

How was Helen going to make a living now? One possibility was to go on stage as a vaudeville entertainer. Pride had prevented her from appearing in these variety shows that included comedy routines, dancing dogs and jugglers. But the pay was good so she signed up.

Vaudeville was noisy and exhausting — and Helen loved it. Audiences adored her, and she always had clever answers for their questions. "Do you close your eyes when you sleep?" someone asked. Helen responded, "I guess I do, but I never stayed awake to see."

In November 1921, two hours before she was to go on stage in Los Angeles, Helen received word that her mother had died. Helen was heartbroken — she'd grown very close to her mother in the last few years — but she still performed that night. Later that year, during a show in Toronto, Annie became very ill. Polly was forced to take her place on stage that night, and the next year she took over for Annie completely.

By 1923, audiences were no longer crowding the theaters to see vaudeville. Once more, it was time for Helen to think of a new way to make a living.

During their vaudeville tours, Helen and Annie crossed Canada and the United States, performing with acrobats, strongmen, tap dancers and trained seals.

"Life is either a daring adventure or nothing."
— Helen

Helen thought the movie *Deliverance* would be a straightforward retelling of her life, but the filmmakers added dream sequences and other weird scenes.

Well-dressed, young and beautiful, Helen didn't look at all like most people's idea of a person who is deaf and blind.

Annie, Polly and I loved to wear beautiful clothes.

The 8th Wonder of the World
Helen Keller
IN THE PHOTO-PLAY BEAUTIFUL—
"DELIVERANCE"

TREMONT TEMPLE

While in Hollywood, Helen met many of the first movie stars, including the great comic actor Charlie Chaplin (beside Helen), Mary Pickford and Douglas Fairbanks.

During their 20-minute vaudeville act, Helen and Annie talked about how Helen had learned to communicate.

Cross-country fundraiser

With Polly's help, Helen enjoyed playing croquet. She loved being outside where she could feel the rush of the wind and the warmth of the sun.

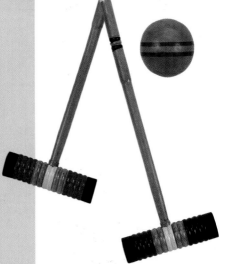

Since 1921, the American Foundation for the Blind (AFB) had been helping people with visual impairments, providing education and other assistance. But this work took money, and the organization needed someone energetic and appealing to help them raise it. The AFB immediately thought of Helen.

Helen was excited by the challenge and agreed to try to raise $2 million in six months. Annie and Helen would receive $2000 per month to make four appearances a week. They'd talk about Helen's life, answer questions and ask for donations to the AFB.

People loved seeing Helen and Annie and eagerly gave money. Henry Ford, founder of the Ford Motor Company, contributed generously. Famous writer and broadcaster Will Rogers asked listeners to his national radio show to donate to their cause. At one event, Helen and Annie raised $21 000 — an amazing amount of money for that time.

But it was tiring work. "For three years we traveled the country from coast to coast," wrote Helen. "We addressed 250 000 people at 249 meetings in 123 cities." As Helen watched Annie get weaker and lose her vision, she felt guilty about the effect their exhausting lifestyle had on her teacher. However, she and Annie continued to work hard fundraising for the AFB until 1927.

For years, Helen's publisher had been urging her to write another book about her life. Her first one, *The Story of My Life*, had sold incredibly well. But first, Helen wanted to write about her Swedenborgian religious beliefs because they meant so much to her. *My Religion* was published in 1927. In it she wrote, "All about me is silence and darkness, yet within me, in the spirit, is music and brightness …" Helen's religion helped her through many difficult times in her life.

Annie was now in her 60s and was increasingly losing her sight and health. In 1930, Helen thought a trip to Ireland, the home of Annie's parents, and England would help. But Annie felt desperate and hopeless. During their travels, Helen had to become her teacher's guide — and try to give her the same help and encouragement Annie had given her.

"When we do the best we can, we never know what miracle is wrought in our life, or in the life of another." — Helen

Midstream: My Later Life *was published in 1929. I found writing hard work, but my books sold well.*

Helen loved all forms of art, but sculpture was the one she could most appreciate since she could touch it and experience it.

Helen and Annie worked hard raising money for the AFB. Some days they made five speeches. Money poured in, and sometimes hundreds of people had to be turned away from their appearances.

As well as raising money to help people who were blind, Helen wanted to raise the world's awareness of their needs. Even when she was busy giving speeches, she made time to visit schools for children who were deaf and blind.

Life without Teacher

"When one door of happiness closes, another opens; but often we look so long at the closed door that we do not see the one which has opened for us."
— Helen

American President Franklin D. Roosevelt admired Helen and said, "Anything Helen Keller is for, I am for." Helen met all the presidents from Grover Cleveland to John F. Kennedy.

When Helen, Annie and Polly returned from their two-year tour of England and Ireland, Helen began fundraising for the American Foundation for the Blind (AFB) again. This time, Polly toured with her — Annie stayed home away from the hustle and bustle of life on the road. Helen and Polly spoke at 80 meetings but raised only $20 000. In the 1930s, the United States was in the grip of the Great Depression, and people had little money to spare.

Helen also campaigned to make braille the only system of reading and writing for people with vision loss. Earlier, four other systems were being used. This caused confusion and made it tough for people who were blind to communicate with each other. Thanks to Helen's work, braille became the standard system around the world in 1932.

In June the next year, Helen, Annie and Polly traveled to Scotland for a break. Annie was becoming weaker and weaker and more discouraged about her failing eyesight. While Annie rested, Helen read, wrote articles and began work on a book about her teacher.

The three women returned to Forest Hills in the fall of 1934, but Annie was still despairing and rebellious due to her almost total blindness. She lacked Helen's determination and talent for overcoming obstacles. An eye operation the next spring was a failure. Helen continued raising funds and awareness for the AFB, but also took Annie for holidays in Jamaica and Quebec, hoping she might recover her strength. Nothing helped.

In August 1936, Annie suffered a stroke. Two months later, she drifted into a coma. As Helen sat by her bed, holding her hand, Annie quietly died. Annie was cremated, and her ashes were placed in a memorial at the National Cathedral in Washington, D.C. She was the first woman to be honored like this.

Helen was devastated by Annie's death. Not only had she lived with Annie for almost 50 years, but she also felt that Annie had sacrificed her life to help Helen. Many people believed that now Helen would retire and live with her sister, Mildred, in Alabama. But Helen wanted to continue working and helping other people, with loyal Polly at her side.

With braille finally accepted as the reading and writing system for all people who were blind, more books and magazines could be made available more easily, since they had to be translated into only one system.

b c d e f g h i
k l m n o p q r
t u v w x y z

an you read this sentence?

Just a few days before she died, Annie said, "Thank God I gave up my life that Helen might live. God help her to live without me when I go."

By touching a singer's lips, I could "hear" his voice and enjoy the beauty of the music.

Helen, Annie and Polly loved animals, especially dogs, and almost always had one or two with them.

World traveler

"Alone we can do so little; together we can do so much."
— Helen

When Helen visited South Africa in February 1951, the Zulus gave her the name Homvuselelo, which means "you have aroused the consciences of many."

Traveling the world helped me draw attention to the needs of people who were deaf, blind or deaf-blind.

After Annie's death, Helen became more determined to share her message of peace with the world. She also wanted to let everyone know the important contributions people with disabilities can make to society. In 1937, she and Polly toured Japan, giving 97 lectures in 39 cities. They received many gifts, including a purebred Akita dog, the first to be imported into the United States.

In 1939, Helen and Polly moved to Westport, Connecticut. The women couldn't travel to other countries during World War II (1939–1945), but Helen spent her time writing and visiting American soldiers who'd been wounded in the war.

After the war, Helen and Polly traveled the world again. Helen became a counselor on international relations for the American Foundation for Overseas Blind in 1946. She and Polly visited 35 countries between 1946 and 1957. Wherever they went, they visited people who were blind and tried to understand what they really needed.

Their European tour had barely begun when Helen and Polly received word that their Connecticut home had burned to the ground. Helen accepted the news bravely — despite learning that her love letters from Peter Fagan had been destroyed, as well as the book about Annie that she'd been writing for six years. The two women had a new house built on the site of the old one and moved in just 10 months after the terrible fire. But it took Helen nine years to rewrite her book on Annie.

Helen had been famous around the world for almost as long as she could remember. But she never let her fame go to her head. Although Eleanor Roosevelt, the former U.S. president's wife, called her "America's goodwill ambassador to the world," Helen called herself "an international beggar."

Helen was 73 years old when she toured Latin America in 1953. Her fingers were becoming less sensitive and she had to warm them before she could read braille. Despite her aches and pains, in 1955 she began a five-month-long tour through Asia.

The touring and speech-making were tough on Helen, but she knew she was helping change the lives of millions of people with visual impairments around the world. She brought them courage and hope. And, thanks to her visits, many real improvements became available — such as better job training, more braille books and books on tape.

By standing in the midst of dancers, Helen could feel them whirl around her and "see" them dancing.

Helen felt her first Akita dog, Kami, knew how she felt. "If I cried from loneliness for my beloved teacher," said Helen, "he would ... lick away the tears." Here she is with her second Akita, Kenzan Go.

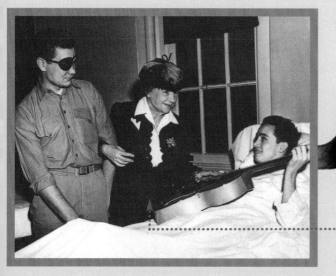

Visiting wounded World War II soldiers was "the crowning experience of my life," claimed Helen.

Looking toward the future

"I seldom think about my limitations, and they never make me sad. Perhaps there is just a touch of yearning at times, but it is vague, like a breeze among flowers." — Helen

The Unconquered (later called *Helen Keller in Her Story*) won an Oscar for best documentary film in 1955.

Despite Helen's bad experience filming *Deliverance* years before, she was pleased to star in *The Unconquered*, a documentary movie about her life made in the early 1950s. Helen and Annie's story also inspired the 1956 television show, "The Miracle Worker," which later became a popular play and an award-winning movie.

In 1957, Polly had a stroke and was no longer able to look after Helen. Evelyn Seide from the American Foundation for the Blind and nurse Winifred Corbally took over Helen's care. After Polly died in 1960, with Helen at her side, her ashes were placed next to Annie's at the National Cathedral in Washington.

Helen was now 80 years old. Polly had been with her for almost 50 years, and Helen found it tough to carry on without her. When Helen had a stroke in 1961, it took her a long time to recover. She often seemed to think she was back living with Teacher and John Macy. Helen didn't appear in public again, but she continued to receive awards from around the world.

Helen suffered a heart attack at the end of May 1968. A few days later, she died in her sleep. At her funeral, every word was translated into sign language so that all her friends who were hard of hearing could take part in the service. Later, Helen's ashes were placed beside Annie's and Polly's.

The benefits of Helen's life of hard work are still felt around the world. Back in 1925, she'd challenged the Lions Club International to help her battle against vision loss. That organization is still known worldwide for its work for people who are blind. As well, in 1988 the Helen Keller Foundation for Research and Education was started in response to Helen's request: "Help me to hasten the day when there shall be no blindness."

Every year, organizations around the world celebrate Helen Keller Day on her birthday, June 27. Helen's bravery makes people think about the importance of courage, determination and hope. Her achievements force the world to see people with disabilities differently. Helen's story still challenges people everywhere to dream great dreams and never give up.

When Helen turned 80 years old, she was asked about her future plans. "I will always — as long as I have breath — work for the handicapped," she replied.

Helen would be pleased with the many groups today that help visually impaired people. For instance, some organizations provide glasses to needy kids with poor vision.

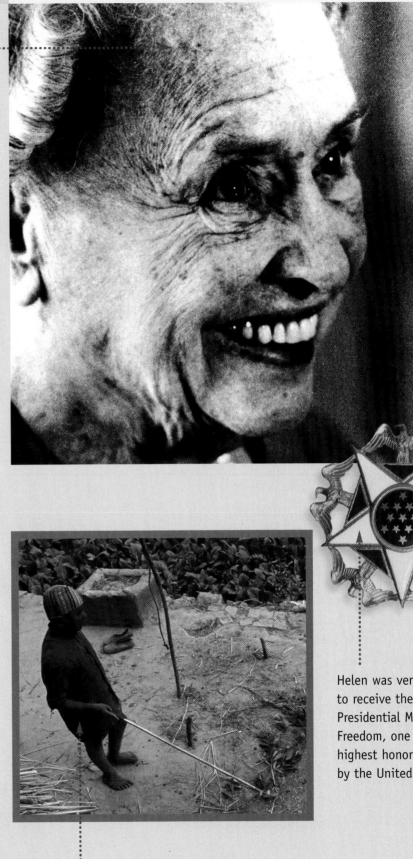

Helen Keller Worldwide works hard to prevent blindness, restore vision and help visually impaired people.

Helen Keller
WORLDWIDE

Programs around the world teach blind people how to get jobs and live with their disability. This boy in Nepal is learning how to use a cane.

Helen was very proud to receive the Presidential Medal of Freedom, one of the highest honors given by the United States.

Helen's life at a glance

1866 April 14 — Anne "Annie" Mansfield Sullivan is born in Feeding Hills, part of Agawam, Massachusetts

1880 June 27 — Helen Adams Keller is born in Tuscumbia, Alabama

1882 At the age of 19 months, Helen loses her sight and hearing as a result of an illness

1886 Helen and her father meet with Alexander Graham Bell. He recommends they write to Boston's Perkins Institution for the Blind to find a teacher for Helen

1887 March 3 — Annie arrives in Tuscumbia to become Helen's teacher

April 5 — Helen has a breakthrough when Annie finger-spells "W-A-T-E-R" into Helen's hand while pumping water

1888 Helen begins attending the Perkins Institution (now the Perkins School) for the Blind and stays for about four years

1890 Helen receives speech lessons at the Horace Mann School for the Deaf (now the Horace Mann School for the Deaf and Hard of Hearing) in Boston

1891 Helen sends Michael Anagnos her story "The Frost King" and is later accused of plagiarism

1893 Helen, Annie and Alexander Graham Bell spend three weeks at the World's Fair in Chicago, Illinois

1894 October — Helen begins studying speech at the Wright-Humason School for the Deaf in New York City

1896 August 19 — Helen's father dies

Helen chooses Swedenborgianism for her religion

October — Helen attends the Cambridge School for Young Ladies in Boston

1897 Helen studies with a private tutor for two more years to prepare for college entrance exams

1899 July — Helen passes Radcliffe College's entrance exams

1900 September — Helen enters Radcliffe College in Boston

1902 *The Story of My Life* is published as a series of articles

1903 *The Story of My Life* is published as a book

1904 Helen purchases a farm at Wrentham, Massachusetts

June 28 — Helen graduates with honors from Radcliffe. She is the first college graduate who is deaf-blind

1905 May 2 — Annie marries John Albert Macy

1908 Helen publishes *The World I Live In*

1910 Helen has her eyes removed and replaced with glass eyes

1913–1916 Helen and Annie cross the United States on a series of lecture tours

1913 *Out of the Dark* is published

1914 Polly Thomson joins Helen and Annie on their lecture tour

John Macy leaves Annie but they never officially divorce

1915 The organization Permanent Blind Relief War Fund (now Helen Keller Worldwide) is founded

1916 Helen and Peter Fagan fall in love but Helen's family won't let them marry

1917 Helen, Annie and Polly move to Forest Hills, New York

1919 Helen stars in the movie *Deliverance*

1919–1923 Helen, Annie and Polly tour with a vaudeville show

1921 November 20 — Helen's mother dies

1924 Helen begins fundraising for the American Foundation for the Blind

1927 Helen publishes *My Religion*

1929 *Midstream: My Later Life* is published

1930 Helen, Annie and Polly travel to England and Ireland

1932 Braille is accepted as the world's standard alphabet for people with vision loss, thanks largely to Helen's work

1933 Helen, Annie and Polly visit Scotland

1936 October 20 — Annie dies in Forest Hills

1937 Helen and Polly tour Japan. Helen gives 97 lectures in 39 cities

1938 *Helen Keller's Journal: 1936–1937* is published

1939 Helen and Polly move to Westport, Connecticut

1940 Helen publishes *Let Us Have Faith*

1943 Helen begins visiting hospitals to meet soldiers who are blind, deaf and wounded

1946 The American Foundation for Overseas Blind (now part of Helen Keller Worldwide) appoints Helen counselor on international relations

Helen tours England, France, Greece and Italy. Her home in Westport is destroyed by fire

1948 Helen tours Australia, Japan and New Zealand

Polly has her first stroke

1951 Helen and Polly tour South Africa

1952 Helen is given the Gold Medal of the National Institute of Social Sciences in the United States (given each year to a distinguished person who has been of outstanding service to humanity)

Helen and Polly tour Egypt, Israel, Jordan, Lebanon and Syria

In a ceremony commemorating Louis Braille, Helen is made a Chevalier of the Legion of Honor, France's highest honor

1953 Helen and Polly travel through Brazil, Chile, Mexico, Panama and Peru

1954 The movie *The Unconquered*, later renamed *Helen Keller in Her Story*, is released

1955 *Helen Keller in Her Story* wins an Academy Award for best feature-length documentary

Helen publishes *Teacher: Anne Sullivan Macy*

Helen tours India and Japan

Helen becomes the first woman to receive an honorary degree from Harvard University

1956 The show "The Miracle Worker" is broadcast on television. It's later made into a play (1959) and a movie (1962)

1957 Helen publishes *The Open Door*

Helen and Polly tour Denmark, Finland, Iceland, Norway and Sweden

1960 March 21 — Polly Thomson dies at Westport

1961 Helen suffers her first stroke

1964 Helen is awarded the Presidential Medal of Freedom by President Lyndon Johnson

1968 June 1 — Helen dies at Westport

Visit Helen

● ● ●▶ **Ivy Green,** Tuscumbia, Alabama

Visit Helen's birthplace, tour the home and gardens and see the water pump where she first learned to communicate. At the Helen Keller Festival every year at the end of June, you can try learning braille and sign language and see the play *The Miracle Worker* about Helen and Annie.

● ● ●▶ **Alexander Graham Bell National Historic Site,** Baddeck, Nova Scotia

Find out about Alexander Graham Bell's inventions and his work with people with hearing impairments. Helen often visited Bell at his nearby home, and you can see photos of them together and learn about their friendship.

● ● ●▶ **Perkins School for the Blind,** Watertown, Massachusetts

Tour the Perkins School for the Blind. (Helen went to Perkins when it was still in Boston.) You'll also find out about the students who attend the school today and the technology that helps them. (Be sure to call ahead to schedule your tour.)

You can visit my first home and Perkins School and find out more about my friend, Dr. Bell.

Index